An Appleseed Editions book

First published in 2005 by Franklin Watts
96 Leonard Street, London, EC2A 4XD

Franklin Watts Australia
Level 17/207 Kent Street, Sydney, NSW 2000

© 2005 Appleseed Editions

Created by Appleseed Editions Ltd,
Well House, Friars Hill, Guestling, East Sussex,
TN35 4ET

Designed by Guy Callaby

ISBN 0 7496 5991 2

A CIP catalogue for this book is available from the
British Library.

Photographs by Corbis (Archivo Iconografico S.A.,
Bettmann, Jonathan Blair, Barnabas Bosshart, Paul C.
Chauncey, Christie's Images, COLLART HERVE /
CORBIS SYGMA, Seamus Colligan / ZUMA, Dean
Conger, Robert Estall, Macduff Everton, Jack Fields,
Colin Garratt; Milepost 92 1/2, Paul Hardy, Brownie
Harris, Chris Hellier, Angelo Hornak, Hulton-Deut-
sch Collection, Lake County Museum, Charles &
Josette Lenars, Dennis Marsico, Maurice Nimmo;
Frank Lane Picture Agency, Jose Fueste Raga,
Charles O'Rear, Scheufler Collection, Denis Scott,
Richard Hamilton Smith, Joseph Sohm: Visions of
America, Paul A. Souders, James Sparshatt, Staple-
ton Collection, Mark L. Stephenson, ZUMA), Getty
Images (David Bassett, Hulton Archive, Michael
Rosenfield)

Printed in Thailand

CONTENTS

INTRODUCTION

Iron is a silvery-grey metal that is widely found throughout the Earth's crust. It is not found in a pure, ready-made state, but has to be extracted from ores that are obtained from different kinds of rocks.

The chemical symbol for iron is Fe, which comes from the Latin word for the metal, ferrum. It was already an important material by the time of the ancient Romans, and hundreds of years later it played a vital role in the Industrial Revolution. Iron is reasonably easy to obtain, can be hammered and moulded into shape, and yet is very strong. This made it very useful in the making of tools and weapons in ancient times, and more recently for transport vehicles such as the 'iron horse', or railway engine. Today, it is still the basic material for many manufactured items and is especially important as the basis of a very strong alloy — steel.

These iron gates at Hampton Court Palace, near London, were made around 1700 by French designer Jean Tijou. They show how iron can be both decorative and practical.

Reactive metal

As far as practical use is concerned, iron has one major disadvantage – it is a highly reactive metal. That is to say, it reacts easily with oxygen to form iron oxide or rust. When iron comes into contact with damp air or oxygen-rich water, it starts to corrode. This means that it produces a coating of oxide and is slowly destroyed by chemical action. At first the thin oxide layer simply discolours the iron, but over time the rust forms pits and holes. This weakens the metal so that it breaks more easily or even falls apart. The easiest way to protect iron objects from rust is to galvanize them, which involves coating them with a protective layer of zinc.

This old train has been attacked by rust, which has worn the iron away unevenly.

In the blood

Iron is an essential element for all animals and plants. Adult humans have about 3.5 grams of iron in their bodies. About two-thirds of this is found in red blood cells, where it forms part of a protein called haemoglobin. This protein in our blood is responsible for carrying oxygen around the body, making it vitally important – a lack of iron would cause weakness and tiredness. Good sources of iron include red meat, green, leafy vegetables and grains. People who suffer from a lack of haemoglobin can also take pills or liquid drops containing iron.

Red blood cells – seen here through a microscope – pick up oxygen in the lungs and carry it throughout the body.

WHERE IN THE WORLD?

Iron ore deposits are found all over the world. Many were formed billions of years ago, in regions that were once covered by shallow seas. Iron compounds in the water combined with sand and silt to form rocks.

In other areas, molten volcanic rocks produced iron ore as they cooled. All of the world's continents produce iron except Antarctica, which has no permanent inhabitants and no industry. Today, the greatest amounts of iron ore are mined in China, Brazil and Australia. Much of this ore is exported to other countries before being turned into iron. China is also the world's leading producer of both iron and steel, followed by Japan, the United States and Russia.

134-D—Open Pit Iron Ore Mine

7B-H1288

PHOTO BY ROLEFF

Mesabi Iron Range, Northern Minnesota

In the late 19th century, iron ore was found in the Mesabi Range of northeastern Minnesota. Many mines were opened, and some are still in production today.

Ironbridge

Ironbridge Gorge, on the Severn River in the West Midlands of England, was named after its most famous landmark – the world's first iron bridge. It was built in 1779 by Abraham Darby III, grandson of the iron manufacturer who built the first coke-fired blast furnace 70 years earlier in nearby Coalbrookdale. In the late 18th century, there were many furnaces, factories and workshops along this stretch of the Severn, making it one of Europe's busiest rivers. This single bridge had a great influence on both technology and architecture. Today, there are several iron museums near the famous bridge and the old ironworks.

The first iron bridge still stands today, spanning 30 metres across the Severn River. Its five curving arch ribs were each cast in two halves, and the bridge used a total of nearly 400 tonnes of cast iron.

The control room of a large steelworks in China.

Shanghai

The northeastern provinces of China saw the greatest development in iron mining and production. Then, much of the industry moved to the city of Shanghai, which lies near the mouth of the great Chang Jiang River. There iron and steel could be manufactured and shipped, both upriver into central China and overseas across the East China Sea. In recent years, the city has developed a new industrial zone with many factories and high-rise apartments for workers and their families.

ORES

Iron is the second-most plentiful metal in the Earth's crust (after aluminium). It makes up about five per cent of the crust and is found in several different ores. The richest iron ores are called haematite and magnetite. They are both iron oxides, and each is made up of more than two-thirds iron.

Although iron is still plentiful in the world, improved techniques have meant that mining companies spend more time and money processing ores containing less iron. Limonite, which is made up of more than half iron, also contains water. This brownish ore is often called 'bog iron' because it is found in marshy ground. Pyrite has a shiny yellow appearance and is known as 'fool's gold' because it is often mistaken for the precious metal. Other common ores are siderite (named after the Greek word for iron) and taconite (named after the Taconic Mountains in the northeastern US).

Iron-ore rocks, like these from Brazil, often look rusty.

Blood-like stone

Haematite is the most common commercial source of iron. Its name means 'blood-like', and some haematite is brownish or dark red in colour. When haematite rocks are scratched, they show a blood-red mark. Large deposits of haematite have been found in North America, South America and Australia. In areas where grains of the ore colour layers of sandstone or shale, the rocks are known as 'red beds'. Where the iron oxide mixes with clay and sand, it also makes a pigment called red ochre. Very hard, compact pieces of haematite can also be polished and used as jewellery.

The haematite used in jewellery usually looks black, but it still produces a red streak if scratched or rubbed against something.

Lodestone

Magnetite is a hard black rock that is different from other ores because it is magnetic. Its name comes from Magnesia, a region in ancient Asia Minor (modern Turkey), where it was once found. According to an ancient Greek legend, a shepherd was amazed to find that the iron tip of his staff clung to some rocks over which he was walking – and discovered magnetite. Around 585 BC, the Greek philosopher Thales of Miletus said that this magnetic stone attracted iron because it had a soul. Hundreds of years later, scientists realized that a piece of magnetite would point north when hung from a string. They called it 'lodestone', and it was used in the earliest compasses.

The Italian island of Elba has much magnetite. Sailors once believed that it was dangerous to sail near the coast of Calamita. This was probably because the island affected a ship's compass in strange ways.

MINING

The various iron ores are mined both underground and at the Earth's surface. Today, most of the world's iron comes from so-called opencast or open-pit mines, where metal is recovered from thick beds of ore that lie close to the surface.

Drills and explosives are used to break up surface rocks, and miners then operate power shovels to dig the material and load it into huge trucks. Open mines are dug in a series of horizontal layers called benches, and roads connect them up to the surface level. The mines are often very large, and some make a hole in the ground more than 150 metres deep. They are often grouped together in iron-rich regions, such as the mountains of Western Australia.

This South African mine is at a place called Thabazimbi, which means 'mountain of iron'. The mine's main ore is haematite.

A drilling machine in the LKAB mine in northern Sweden. Shafts go down 540 metres below the surface, and the mine employs more than 3,000 people.

Underground shafts

In underground mines, vertical shafts are dug down from the surface. Horizontal tunnels then lead off from the shafts to the ore deposits. Miners used to operate drills to remove chunks of ore from the rock face, but today much of this work is done by remote-controlled electric drilling equipment. At Malmberget (meaning 'Ore Mountain'), above the Arctic Circle in northern Sweden, iron ore has been mined since 1892. Today, haematite and magnetite are still dug out from a depth of more than 800 metres, and tourists can visit an old iron-ore mine near the town of Gällivare.

Processing and shipping

When iron-rich ores have reached the processing plant, they are crushed, ground and washed. Less concentrated ores need further processing. Powerful magnets are used to remove particles of magnetite from low-grade ore. Other crushed ores are mixed with liquids, so that iron particles sink to the bottom and can be separated. The particles are then dried and formed into small, round pellets, making them easier to ship and use. In this way, ore with less than a third iron content can be upgraded to pellets that are two-thirds iron. The processing plants are usually next to the mines to save the expense of shipping waste material.

Iron-ore pellets are loaded on to a train in Brazil.

METAL FROM THE SKY

In ancient times, the first people to use iron probably obtained it from fragments of fairly pure metal that they found lying on or buried in the ground. The first metalworkers may have used hard rocks to hammer the iron and perhaps shape it into tools.

We now know that the fragments they found were from meteorites – pieces of metal and rock that come from outer space and crash into Earth's surface. Perhaps ancient people were also aware of this, because in some old languages, the word for iron meant 'metal from the sky'. Modern science has told us that many meteorites are made up of iron and another silvery-white metal called nickel. They probably come from the many rocky asteroids that constantly travel around the sun.

This iron meteorite, weighing more than 30 tonnes, fell in Greenland thousands of years ago. Most meteorites are smashed into small pieces on impact.

Stars and planets

Astronomers believe that many stars are rich in iron, having gobbled up large numbers of asteroids. Many of the planets circling our star (the sun), including Mercury and Venus, have cores made of iron and possibly nickel. Mars has iron oxide (or rust) at its surface, giving it the colour that earned it the nickname 'the Red Planet'. Earth itself has a solid iron core at its very centre, surrounded by an outer core of molten iron and other elements. Iron forms an important part of the solar system and perhaps of the universe as a whole.

The rusty surface of Mars makes it look red. Iron-centred Earth looks blue because it is covered by so much water.

Meteor Crater

The vast Meteor Crater in Arizona is about 1,275 metres wide and 175 metres deep. It was formed up to 50,000 years ago when a huge iron meteorite struck Earth. In 1902, a mining engineer named Daniel Barringer started looking for the buried meteorite, not realizing that it had completely disintegrated on impact. The following year, he formed the Standard Iron Company and claimed mining rights, having found particles of iron mixed with the soil. Scientists later estimated that the Arizona meteorite might have been more than 45 metres across.

Today there is a visitors' centre and museum at Meteor Crater.

THE IRON AGE

Historians often refer to the 'three-age system', which divides prehistoric and ancient time into a series of tool-making periods. Under this system, the Stone Age was followed by the Bronze Age, which led to the Iron Age.

Dates for the ages are not exact, since use of the materials began at different times in various places. Iron from meteorites was used first, and soon after 2,000 BC, the Hittites and other ancient peoples were heating and melting iron ore in order to get the metal from it – a process known as smelting. To the ancient Egyptians and others, iron was at one time more valuable than gold. People in China and India also developed smelting techniques, and ironworking soon spread from southwest Asia to Europe.

These Iron Age axe-heads were found at different locations in Spain. By about 1,000 BC, iron tools had become common throughout southern Europe.

Smelting

Iron was smelted later than copper and tin, the metals that were mixed together to make bronze. This was because iron melts at a much higher temperature (1,535° centigrade) than the other metals, so a fire had to be extremely hot. Early metalworkers used a simple smelting furnace by digging a hole in the ground and building a stone-lined shaft above it. Charcoal was heated in the furnace until it was red-hot, and layers of iron ore were added. When the ore got very hot, it released the metal, which sank to the bottom of the furnace as a bloom, or lump, of iron. The iron could then be reheated and hammered into shape.

This illustration shows a 17th-century Hungarian iron-smelting furnace.

Early ironmasters

The ancient Hittites built an empire in Anatolia (modern Turkey) and were very skilled at making objects from the soft precious metals gold and silver. They were probably the first people to smelt iron, and by 1,400 BC, it had become a very important metal throughout a wider region. Historians believe that it was the Hittites who took iron to ancient Egypt. For use in tools and weapons, the iron had to be hardened by further heating, hammering and plunging into cold water.

This iron dagger sheath dates from the sixth century BC. It is decorated with animal figures.

The Industrial Revolution, which began in Britain during the 18th century, caused huge technological changes throughout the world. The 18th and 19th centuries were a time of great discoveries and inventions, and many of them involved iron.

British ironmakers and engineers led the way, developing new furnaces and processes. In 1784, an English ironmaker named Henry Cort improved the puddling process. This involved stirring molten iron with a long iron bar to cause impurities to burn away. This and other improvements meant that much more – and better – iron was produced. By the early 19th century, iron was being used for many machines, pipes and parts in the factories that were springing up in the world's industrial cities.

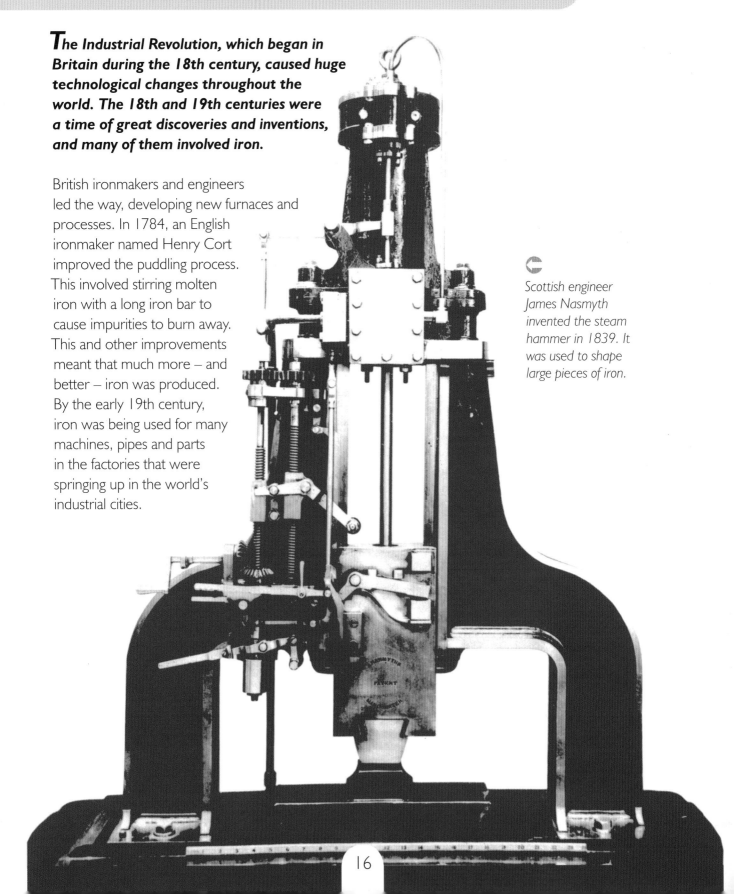

Scottish engineer James Nasmyth invented the steam hammer in 1839. It was used to shape large pieces of iron.

Abraham Darby I – III

In 1709, English ironmaker Abraham Darby (1678–1717) converted a furnace at Coalbrookdale, Shropshire, to burn coke instead of charcoal. He wanted to make iron cheaper and easier to produce so that it could replace brass in the cooking pots he made. Also, wood was needed for making charcoal, and many of the nearby forests had been cleared. Coke was made by heating coal in an airtight oven, and coal was becoming plentiful at that time. Darby's idea worked, and coke soon replaced charcoal for smelting iron. His son, Abraham Darby II (1711–63), went on to improve the quality of the family company's iron. The founder's grandson, Abraham Darby III (1750–91), built the world's first iron bridge.

 This scene of ironworks at Coalbrookdale was painted by Philip James de Loutherbourg in 1808.

Bessemer converter

In the 1850s, British engineer Henry Bessemer (1813–98) invented a new kind of furnace for converting iron into harder, stronger steel. Before that time, steel was little used, because it was difficult and expensive to make. In Bessemer's new process, air was blown through molten iron in a furnace lined with limestone. High temperatures caused impurities in the iron to form slag and removed some of the carbon in the metal. Today's basic steelmaking process is simply an improvement on the original Bessemer converter.

A Bessemer converter in action. The new process, which was patented in 1855, cut the price of steel in half.

WROUGHT AND CAST IRON

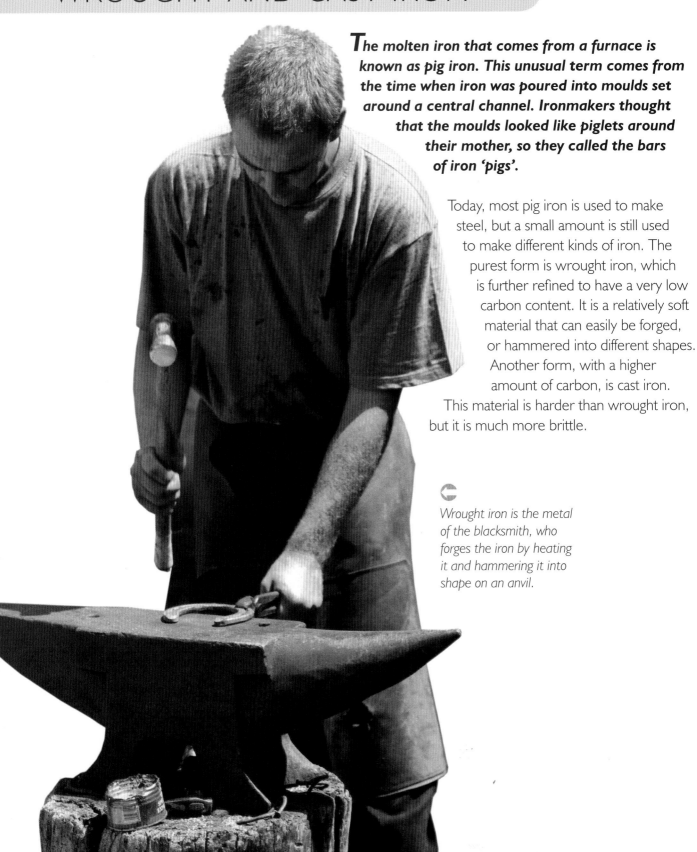

The molten iron that comes from a furnace is known as pig iron. This unusual term comes from the time when iron was poured into moulds set around a central channel. Ironmakers thought that the moulds looked like piglets around their mother, so they called the bars of iron 'pigs'.

Today, most pig iron is used to make steel, but a small amount is still used to make different kinds of iron. The purest form is wrought iron, which is further refined to have a very low carbon content. It is a relatively soft material that can easily be forged, or hammered into different shapes. Another form, with a higher amount of carbon, is cast iron. This material is harder than wrought iron, but it is much more brittle.

Wrought iron is the metal of the blacksmith, who forges the iron by heating it and hammering it into shape on an anvil.

Blast furnace

Today, iron ore is smelted in a blast furnace. This separates the metal from the rock more efficiently than was possible in the old charcoal oven. The furnace is made of steel lined with heat-resistant firebricks. Coke and limestone are fed into the top of the furnace along with the iron ore, and blasts of hot air (preheated to about 1,000° centigrade) are blown into the lower part through nozzles. The coke burns and the limestone combines with the rocky parts of the ore to make slag. This leaves molten metal, which runs off at the bottom as pig iron. The waste slag is also tapped off, and is often broken up to make rubble for building roads.

This blast furnace was photographed at a Russian factory in the 1930s. Iron is smelted as a continuous process, with new materials being added at the top as iron and slag are tapped at the bottom.

At the foundry

Pig iron is delivered to a foundry to make and shape cast iron. There the iron is re-melted in a furnace called a cupola before being cast, or poured, into moulds to make the required shape. If the metal is allowed to cool slowly, it makes soft, tough grey cast iron. But if it is cooled quickly with water, it makes brittle, white cast iron. Mass-produced cast iron became an important building material from the late 18th century until it was replaced by steel.

The Crystal Palace was built for London's Great Exhibition in 1851. It was made of cast iron (with some wrought iron) and glass, with wooden flooring.

STEELMAKING

***S**teel, which is a refined product of iron, has been a very important alloy since the 19th century. It is much older than that, however, and small amounts were made early in the Iron Age. The Haya people of present-day Tanzania, in East Africa, produced steel in shaft furnaces for about 2,000 years.*

Today, most steel is produced in large factories by the basic oxygen process, or BOP. Molten iron is loaded into a furnace along with scrap steel. A lance is lowered into the furnace to blow a jet of oxygen over the molten metal. The oxygen combines with impurities in the metal, and they either form part of the waste slag or exit as exhaust gases. The furnace is then tilted to pour out the molten steel. In an alternative process, a powerful electric current produces the heat needed to turn iron into steel.

An integrated steelworks makes iron in a blast furnace, converts it to steel in a BOP furnace and rolls the steel in mills.

Steel sheets are produced in a rolling mill in Canada.

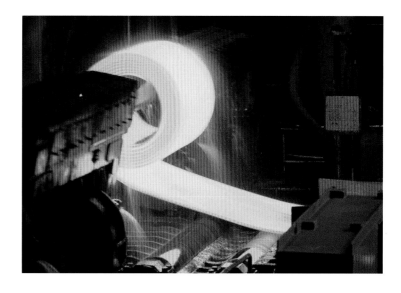

Rolling mills

Molten steel is poured into cast-iron moulds to make ingots or slabs. The slabs are then reheated and passed between heavy rollers that squeeze them into the shapes and sizes required. Many of the hot-rolling mills are very long buildings, because they eventually produce long, thin sheets of steel. Some of these are shaped into rods and bars. At the end of the building, the steel is rolled into a coil. The rolling-mill process also improves the steel by making it stronger and more flexible.

Special steels

There are many different kinds of steel, including galvanized steel, which is coated with zinc in the same way iron is. High-carbon steels are tougher, but they are also more brittle. Stainless steel is used for cutlery, kitchen equipment, and surgical instruments. It is made by adding chromium and nickel to the alloy. Some steel is coated with tin to make the so-called tinplate that is used to make drink cans. Tungsten and cobalt harden and strengthen steel, making it very useful as a material for cutting tools.

Tungsten-steel saws can be used to cut other metals.

TRANSPORTATION

Since the beginning of the 19th century, iron has played a major part in the development of travel and transportation. In 1804, English engineer Richard Trevithick built the world's first steam locomotive. It ran on cast-iron rails, pulling cars from an ironworks near Merthyr Tydfil to a canal 15 kilometres away.

Just over 20 years later, steam trains were carrying their first passengers. In many countries, this new transportation system was known as the 'iron way'. All the early rails were indeed made of iron until the first steel tracks were laid on the London and North Western Railway in 1862. By that time, many ships were also being built of iron, despite the fact that earlier shipbuilders had believed that only wooden vessels would float.

The Forth railway bridge, in Scotland, opened in 1890. It took 55,000 tonnes of steel and 8 million rivets to build the 1,630-metre bridge.

The giant iron hull of the Great Eastern *dwarfs an older wooden vessel. Brunel's ship was driven by both paddle wheels and a propeller.*

Iron hulls

The first iron steamship to go to sea was the *Aaron Manby*, which was built at the Horseley ironworks in central England in 1821. Twenty-two years later, the great British engineer Isambard Kingdom Brunel launched the first of his iron ships, called the *Great Britain*. The ship's hull was made of 1,040 tonnes of iron, and it had a six-bladed iron propeller. Brunel's next ship, the *Great Eastern*, was the largest ship ever built when it was launched in 1858. Its iron hull was 211 metres long, and it was big enough to carry 15,000 tonnes of coal to fire its enormous iron boilers. Most modern ships are made of steel.

Steel shells

The bodies of early cars, including the famous Model T Ford, were made of wood. But manufacturers soon found that iron and steel were much stronger and even cheaper, especially when cars could be mass-produced on long production lines. Today's cars have body shells made of high-strength sheet steel, which is light and very tough. The cars have crumple zones at the front and back, which absorb energy in the event of a crash.

Computer-controlled robots weld steel panels together in a modern car plant.

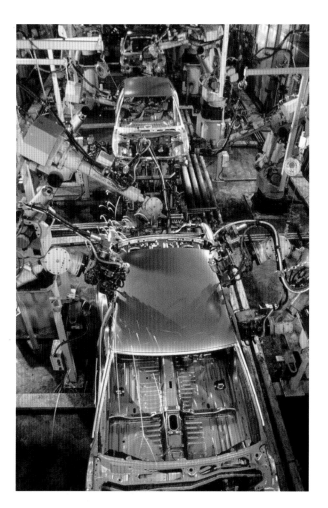

IRON AND STEEL STRUCTURES

In the mid-19th century, architects began using iron for columns, arches and other structural parts of public buildings. This led to the use of iron and steel as the framework for high-rise buildings, especially the new 'skyscrapers' that started to appear in Chicago and other American cities.

Steel rods and wire mesh were also buried inside concrete, making it a very strong building material. Reinforced concrete is still used today for many building projects, including the world's tallest skyscrapers, the Taipei 101 office block in Taiwan (508 metres high) and the twin Petronas Towers in Kuala Lumpur, Malaysia (452 metres). Steel girders are also used as a framework for buildings, towers, bridges and many other large structures. The deck of the biggest suspension bridge in the world, the Akashi Kaikyo Bridge in Japan, is held up by steel wires with a total length of 300,000 kilometres!

The wrought-iron Eiffel Tower was built in Paris for the World's Fair of 1889. Its designer, Gustave Eiffel, wanted to name it the '300-metre Tower'. Today, with its antenna on top, it is 321 metres tall. The iron structure is repainted every five years.

Stainless-steel monument

The tallest monument in the U.S., the Gateway Arch in St. Louis, Missouri, commemorates the city's important role as a gateway to the settlement of the West. Designed by Finnish-American architect Eero Saarinen, the arch was built between 1961 and 1965. Its triangular outer surface is made of 6-millimetre thick stainless steel, with an inner skin of carbon steel and reinforced concrete and steel stiffeners between them. Small lift cars carry visitors up the hollow interior to an observation area at the top of the arch.

Millennium wheel

The London Eye observation wheel was put up beside the River Thames in 1999 to celebrate the new millennium. With its rim, spokes and supporting frame made of steel, the Eye reaches a height of 135 metres. The 23-metre spindle in the middle of the wheel is also made of cast steel. It was too big to cast in one piece, so it was made in eight smaller sections. The wheel takes about 30 minutes to revolve once, turning slowly enough for passengers to get on and off while it keeps moving.

The Gateway Arch is exactly as high as it is wide – 192 metres. More than 800 tonnes of stainless steel plate were used in its construction.

Passengers on the London Eye have a view of up to 40 kilometres on a clear day. The capsules remain horizontal as the wheel turns.

USEFUL RESOURCE

Most of today's iron is used to make steel alloys, but there are still some uses left for iron objects. Cast iron is used to make things such as manhole covers and engine blocks for cars.

The old kitchen appliances that were once made of cast iron are now generally made of stainless steel. Wrought iron is mainly used for ornamental work, such as decorative railings and gates and specialized pieces of sculpture. In addition to its use in construction and transportation, steel has replaced iron in the making of tools and machines. Engines, gears, crankshafts and many other mechanical parts are usually made of steel.

A farrier shoes a horse. Today most horseshoes are made of steel.

In the home

Household appliances such as washing machines, dishwashers and refrigerators are all made from coated steel sheet. Since most are painted white, they are sometimes called 'white goods'. Inside the machines, the sheet used is made from stainless steel to prevent rusting. This is also used for pans, kettles, cutlery and kitchen sinks, making them hygienic and easy to clean. Years ago many of these items were made of iron.

Stainless steel is a very popular material for kitchen accessories and cookware. It is strong, looks good, does not contaminate food and is easy to clean.

Julio González made Woman Seated II *from wrought iron in 1935 – 36.*

Art material

Spanish artist Julio González (1876–1942) has been called the founding father of iron sculpture. González learned metalwork from his father, who was a goldsmith and sculptor. In 1900, the young artist moved to Paris, where he became a friend of Pablo Picasso (1881–1973). Some years later, Picasso asked González to teach him the techniques of forging and welding iron. In the early 1930s, both artists made many pieces out of wrought iron that influenced later sculptors. Picasso even used pieces of scrap iron, springs, saucepan lids and bolts that he found lying around. American sculptor Alexander Calder (1898–1976) also worked in iron, often painting his finished works.

TODAY AND TOMORROW

World production of iron is at an all-time high today, and there does not appear to be any shortage of reserves. At the same time, recycling methods have improved, helping to ensure that the demand for steel and other ferrous metals is met.

Factories and foundries are trying to produce steel more efficiently, controlling production with the use of computers. Today it takes 40 per cent less energy to produce a tonne of steel than it did in 1970. Researchers are developing new, lightweight steels for cars and other items, and scientists continue looking for new production processes for iron, steel, and other ferrous metals. These developments are welcomed by environmentalists, who are concerned that an increase in mines and factories may spoil the land.

The 180-metre Swiss Re Tower, nicknamed 'the Gherkin', opened in London in 2004. Like other modern skyscrapers, its framework is made of steel.

Recycling ferrous scrap

There are three kinds of ferrous scrap, or waste iron and steel. Home or mill scrap is produced within steelworks and can easily be reused in the furnace. New or industrial scrap returns to the steelworks from factories that make products from steel, such as washing-machine manufacturers. Old or post-consumer scrap is made up of goods that have been discarded after serving their purpose, especially cars, appliances and cans. Many countries now have recycling programmes, and in nations such as Britain, more than three-quarters of ferrous scrap is recycled. Throughout the world, steel is the most recycled metal.

Protecting the environment

Mining ore, processing iron and manufacturing steel goods all have an impact on the environment. Many governments have introduced laws to reduce pollution. For example, iron-ore mines next to Lake Superior used to dump waste into the lake, the largest freshwater body in the world. This was finally stopped by law, and the mines now have their own artificial basins, which are carefully controlled and regularly checked. In Brazil, iron and other metals have been found within the Amazon rainforest. Environmentalists are working hard to keep the world's largest rainforest from being ruined by mining activities, including the building of roads and railways.

At a scrapyard, cars are broken up by a shredder, and the metal is separated from other materials. Then presses crush the scrap metal into small bundles ready to be delivered back to a steelworks.

Iron, gold, copper, and other metals are being mined in the Amazon rain forest. Trees are cleared to make space and to provide fuel.

GLOSSARY

alloy   A mixture of two or more metals.

anvil   A heavy iron block on which metals can be hammered and shaped.

asteroid   A small rocky body that travels around the sun.

astronomer   Someone who studies stars, planets and other objects in space.

bench   A horizontal layer or flat ledge in an opencast mine.

blacksmith   A person who makes and repairs iron objects.

bloom   A small mass of iron.

cast iron   Hard, brittle iron that is cast in a mould.

charcoal   A black form of carbon made by heating wood.

coke   A solid fuel made from coal.

compound   Something made by combining two or more different things.

continent   One of Earth's seven huge land masses.

core   The central part of something.

corrode   To be slowly destroyed by chemical action.

crust   Earth's outer layer.

cupola   A furnace for refining metals.

element   A substance that cannot be separated into a simpler form.

environmentalist   A person who is concerned about and acts to protect the natural environment.

export   To send goods to another country for sale.

extract   To take out or obtain something from a source.

farrier   A blacksmith who shoes horses.

ferrous metal   A metal that contains iron.

firebrick   A brick that can withstand great heat.

forge   To shape metal by heating and then hammering it.

foundry   A workshop where metals are cast.

furnace   An oven-like structure in which materials can be heated to very high temperatures.

galvanize   To coat (iron or steel) with a protective layer of the silvery-white metal zinc.

girder   A large iron or steel beam.

haemoglobin A protein in red blood cells that carries oxygen around the body.

Industrial Revolution The rapid development of machinery, factories and industry that began in the late 18th century.

ingot A rectangular mould used for casting metals.

ironworks A place where iron is smelted or iron goods are made.

lodestone A piece of the iron ore magnetite, often used as a magnet.

low-grade Of low content or quality.

meteorite A piece of metal or rock that falls to Earth's surface from outer space.

opencast or **open-pit mine** A mine in which ore is extracted at or near the surface of the earth.

ore Rock or mineral containing a useful metal.

pig iron Crude iron obtained from a furnace and moulded into oblong blocks.

pollution Damage caused to the environment by harmful substances.

precious metal One of the valuable metals – gold, silver or platinum.

protein A substance that forms part of body tissues and helps the body live and grow.

puddling Stirring molten iron to make it more pure.

reactive Describing a metal that reacts easily with the air or another substance (and corrodes).

recycle To process used material so that it can be used again.

rivet A metal pin or bolt for holding metal plates together.

scrap Waste metal.

silt A fine layer of mud and clay.

slag Stony waste matter that is produced when ore is smelted.

smelt To heat and melt ore to get metal from it.

steelworks A factory where steel is made.

tinplate Sheet steel coated with a thin layer of tin.

weld To join metal pieces together by heating and pressing.

wrought iron Tough, relatively soft iron that can easily be hammered into shape.

INDEX